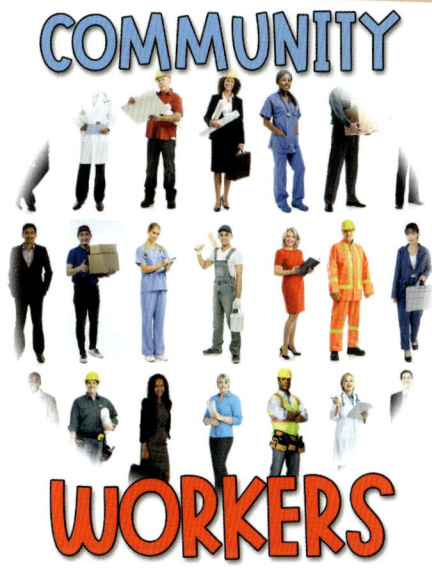

COMMUNITY WORKERS

Written By: Anna DiGilio

All rights reserved. No part of this publication may be reproduced, distributed, or transmitted in any form or by any means, including photocopying, recording, or other electronic or mechanical methods, without the prior written permission of the publisher, except in the case of brief quotations embodied in critical reviews and certain other noncommercial uses permitted by copyright law.

For permission requests, write to the publisher:
Laprea Publishing
info@lapreapublishing.com

Website: www.GuidedReaders.com

ISBN: 978-1-64579-045-7

© 2019 Anna DiGilio
www.SimplySkilledTeaching.com

Printed in the United States of America

TABLE OF CONTENTS

Communities .... Page 4

Keeping People Safe .... Page 5

Keeping People Healthy .... Page 7

Helping People Learn .... Page 9

Helping People Go Places .... Page 11

Keeping the Community
Clean and Beautiful .... Page 12

Building and Fixing Things .... Page 14

Helping People Connect .... Page 15

Helping with the Government .... Page 16

Children in Communities .... Page 17

Glossary .... Page 18

Communities

A community is a group of people. They live near each other. They work with each other. They help make their community a good place to live.

Keeping People Safe

These community workers put out fires. They save people from buildings that are on fire. They help people who <u>breathe</u> smoke. They help pets, too.

Firefighters

These community workers stop people who break laws. They also help people who are lost or hurt.

Many of these community workers drive a car. Some ride a horse. Others ride a motorcycle. Some work with a police dog.

Police officers

Keeping People Healthy

These community workers help people who are sick or hurt. They find out what hurts. Then they help people get better.

Doctor and patient

These community workers help keep teeth <u>healthy</u>. They fix holes in teeth. They teach people how to take care of their teeth.

Dentist with patient

Helping People Learn

These community workers help people learn. They help children learn to read, write, and do math. They help children do their best.

Teacher with her students

These community workers help people find books to read. They work in a <u>library</u>. What do you want to learn about? Turtles? Trains? Jungles? Jupiter? Ask this community worker!

Librarian

Helping People Go Places

These community workers take people from place to place. Some of them take children to school. They bring children home after school. They make sure children are safe.

Bus driver

Keeping the Community Clean and Beautiful

These community workers pick up trash. They put it in big trucks. Then they take it away.

Sanitation workers

Landscaper

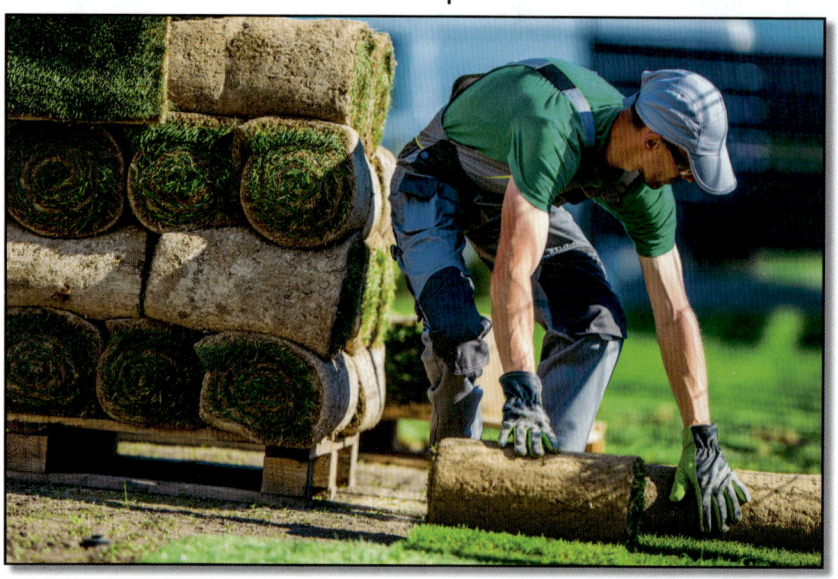

These community workers take care of plants. They help make yards pretty. They also work on plants around schools, parks, and malls. They trim trees, too.

Building and Fixing Things

These community workers do many jobs. Some use big machines. They clear land for new roads or buildings. Some mix <u>concrete</u> or dig <u>tunnels</u>. Others fix roofs or wires.

Construction workers

Helping People Connect

These community workers sort mail at a post office. Then they take letters to people. They take <u>packages</u>, too. They also pick up letters that people want to send.

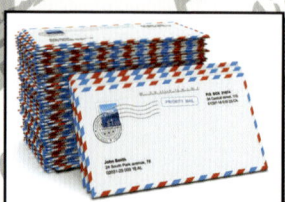  

Mail carrier

Helping With the Government

This community worker is the top person in a community. He or she makes sure the community works right. He or she wants the community to be a safe and great place.

This is the New York City Mayor Bill de Blasio. He took office on January 1, 2014.

Children in Communities

Children are important to a community, too. Your "job" right now is to learn and grow. How does your community help you? How do you help your community?

GLOSSARY

<u>breathe</u>
take in and let out air through the nose or mouth

<u>concrete</u>
a very strong building material made by mixing cement, sand, and broken rocks

<u>healthy</u>
not sick or hurt

<u>library</u>
a place with many books, videos, and other things that people can borrow

GLOSSARY

<u>packages</u>
boxes or things in paper or plastic sent by mail

<u>tunnels</u>
passages that go under the ground